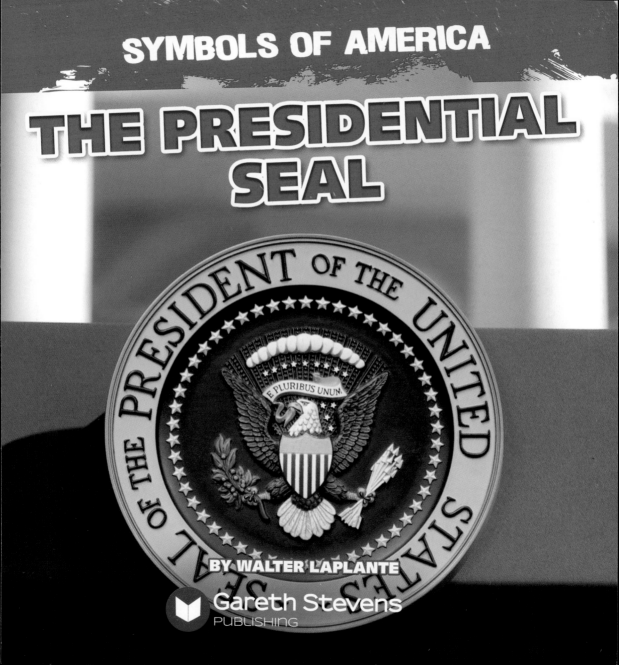

THE PRESIDENTIAL SEAL

BY WALTER LAPLANTE

Gareth Stevens
PUBLISHING

Please visit our website, www.garethstevens.com. For a free color catalog of all our high-quality books, call toll free 1-800-542-2595 or fax 1-877-542-2596.

Library of Congress Cataloging-in-Publication Data

LaPlante, Walter.
The presidential seal / by Walter LaPlante.
p. cm. — (Symbols of America)
Includes index.
ISBN 978-1-4824-1886-6 (pbk.)
ISBN 978-1-4824-1885-9 (6-pack)
ISBN 978-1-4824-1887-3 (library binding)
1. United States — Seal — Juvenile literature. 2. Emblems, National — United States — Juvenile literature. I. Title.
CW15GS 2015
929.9—d23

Published in 2015 by
Gareth Stevens Publishing
111 East 14th Street, Suite 349
New York, NY 10003

Copyright © 2015 Gareth Stevens Publishing

Designer: Sarah Liddell and Laura Bowen
Editor: Kristen Rajczak

Photo credits: Cover, pp. 1, 15, 17 spirit of america/Shutterstock.com; p. 5 Universal Images Group/Getty Images; p. 7 John Parrot/Stocktrek Images/ Getty Images; p. 9 Jim Barber/Shutterstock.com; p. 11 (Millard Fillmore) Kean Collection/Staff/Archive Photos/Getty Images; p. 11 (Fillmore's drawing) Millard Fillmore/Wikimedia Commons; p. 11 (Stabler's drawing) Edward Stabler/ Wikimedia Commons; p. 13 Diane Walker/Contributor/The LIFE Images Collection/ Getty Images; p. 19 (bronze) Keith McIntyre/Shutterstock.com; p. 19 (money) STILLFX/ Shutterstock.com; p. 19 (seal at White House) Chip Somodevilla/Staff/ Getty Images News/Getty Images; p. 19 (on plane) 1000 Words/Shutterstock.com; p. 21 U.S. Government/Wikimedia Commons.

Printed in the United States of America

CPSIA compliance information: Batch #CS15GS: For further information contact Gareth Stevens, New York, New York at 1-800-542-2595.

CONTENTS

Boldface words appear in the glossary.

Showing Freedom

The United States declared **independence** on July 4, 1776. Only a few hours later, it was decided that the new country should have a way to show its freedom. A **coat of arms** was needed for the new nation.

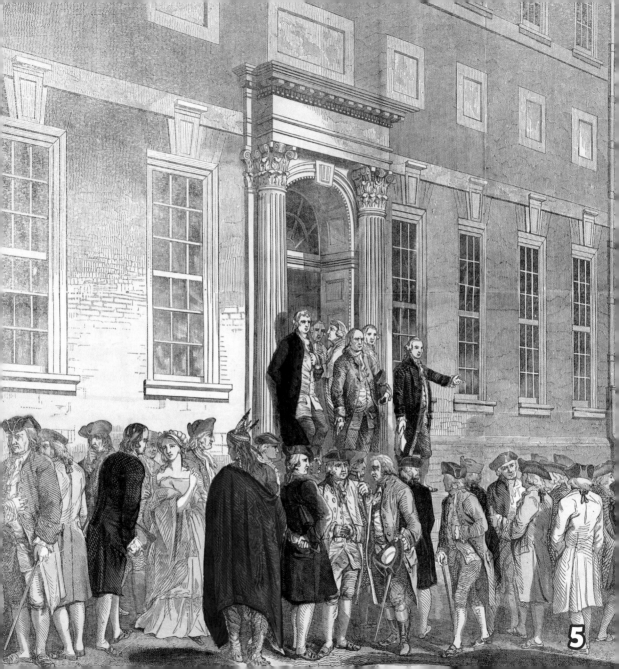

Many Designs

Benjamin Franklin, John Adams, and Thomas Jefferson were the first to work on a **design**. Two other groups created designs for a national **seal**, too. In 1782, a design was chosen. It used parts from the earlier designs.

Today, the Great Seal of the United States is a **symbol** of the United States around the world. It's on government buildings and even money. The Great Seal has two sides. The front is what the presidential seal is based on.

Copycat?

In 1850, President Millard Fillmore wanted a presidential seal to be made. He drew a simple picture of what the seal might look like. But Edward Stabler, who designed the first presidential seal, clearly based it on the Great Seal!

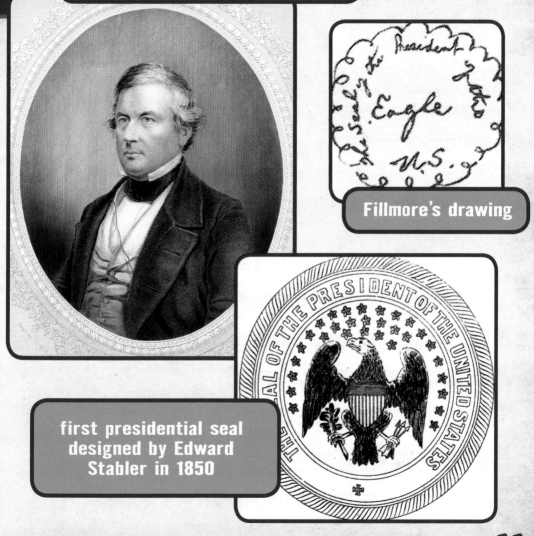

President Millard Fillmore, 1850

Fillmore's drawing

first presidential seal designed by Edward Stabler in 1850

Meaningful

Both seals show the national bird, the bald eagle. It holds a paper in its beak that reads *E pluribus unum*, meaning "out of many, one." These Latin words are a reminder that though there are 50 states, they're all part of one nation.

13

A shield covers the eagle's body. It has 13 red and white stripes, which **represent** the first 13 states. The shield also shows the states' **support** of the president and US government, represented by the blue above the stripes.

15

The eagle holds arrows in its left **talons** and olive branches in its right. The arrows represent war, and the olive branches represent peace. According to an order from President Harry Truman made in 1945, the eagle always faces right, toward peace.

face

olive branches

arrows

17

The Differences

Two features make it easy to tell the presidential seal from the Great Seal. The presidential seal's eagle is on a blue background ringed by 50 stars. The stars are surrounded by the words "Seal of the President of the United States."

THE GREAT SEAL

a bronze plaque

on money

THE PRESIDENTIAL SEAL

at the White House

on the president's plane

Useful Seal

The presidential seal is most important in its **die** form. The president uses a special die for letters to Congress and other papers he signs representing the United States. For this reason, it's a greatly respected US symbol.

THE MAKING OF THE SEAL

JULY 4, 1776

The United States declares its independence. Thomas Jefferson, Benjamin Franklin, and John Adams begin to design the first coat of arms.

1945

President Harry Truman introduces the modern seal.

1850

President Fillmore asks for a presidential seal to be made.

JUNE 20, 1782

The Great Seal is chosen.

GLOSSARY

coat of arms: a design of symbols standing for a family, city, or country

design: the pattern or shape of something. Also, to create a pattern or shape.

die: a tool that creates a mark when pressed into something

independence: freedom

represent: to stand for something else

seal: a symbol or mark of office

support: to hold up and help

symbol: a picture or shape that stands for something else

talon: one of a bird's sharp claws

FOR MORE INFORMATION

BOOKS

Carr, Aaron. *The Great Seal.* New York, NY: AV2 by Weigl, 2014.

Monroe, Tyler. *The Bald Eagle.* North Mankato, MN: Capstone Press, 2014.

WEBSITES

Presidential Seal
americanhistory.si.edu/presidency/5a2a.html
Learn more about each part of the presidential seal on this interactive website.

Symbols of U.S. Government
bensguide.gpo.gov/3-5/symbols/
Read about many other symbols important to the United States.

INDEX